Andrew Goddard and Glynn Harrison

UNWANTED SAME-SEX ATTRACTION
Issues of pastoral and counselling support

Andrew Goddard MA (Oxon), DipTheol, DPhil is Tutor in Christian Ethics at Trinity College Bristol. Ordained in the Church of England, he formerly taught Christian Ethics at Wycliffe Hall, University of Oxford.

Glynn Harrison MD, FRCPsych is Emeritus Professor of Psychiatry, Bristol University. He is a past President of the International Federation of Psychiatric Epidemiology.

The views expressed in this booklet are solely those of the authors and do not claim to represent those of the Christian Medical Fellowship, or any of the academic institutions or other organisations with which the authors are affiliated.

Unwanted Same-Sex Attraction:
Issues of pastoral and counselling support
© 2011 Andrew Goddard and Glynn Harrison

Andrew Goddard and Glynn Harrison have asserted their rights under the Copyright, Design and Patent Act, 1988, to be identified as Authors of this work.

Published by Christian Medical Fellowship
6 Marshalsea Road, London SE1 1HL
www.cmf.org.uk

All rights reserved. No part of this publication may be reproduced or transmitted in any form or by any means, electronic or mechanical, including photocopy, recording or any information storage and retrieval system, without permission in writing from the publisher.

ISBN 978-0-906747-42-1

CONTENTS

PREFACE	5
INTRODUCTION	7
KEY POINTS	9
1. The context and the challenge	13
2. Summary of evidence on the patterning of human sexual desires	17
3. A framework for Christian ministry among people with unwanted same-sex attraction	21
4. Conclusion	29
REFERENCES	31

PREFACE

Whatever the model of 'therapy' or counselling, the relationship between the counsellor and the client has always been regarded as confidential. Two people determine the goals, and that remains between them, undisclosed to anyone else. That is the basis on which 'talking therapies' and counselling work. People seek help for diverse reasons, but the task of the counsellor is always to try to help on the basis of a contract to which both can subscribe.

Helping someone with unwanted same-sex attraction is no different. The counsellor does not come to the interview with an already formed plan. It is based on discussion with the client, what the client wants to achieve and what the counsellor considers to be possible.

Of course all therapists must operate ethically and their work must be grounded in 'best practice'. But our evaluation of the evidence for efficacy needs to be objective, fair and scientifically credible.

Dr Andrew Goddard and Professor Glynn Harrison have approached the issue of assisting those with unwanted same sex attraction through a careful and diligent appraisal of the issues. Their work merits thoughtful attention from all involved in the support of those who struggle with this issue.

Andrew Sims MD FRCPsych
May 2011; Past President, Royal College of Psychiatrists

INTRODUCTION

It is important to be clear from the outset that this paper is not written to convince anyone they should change their view about the morality of same-sex sexual relationships. It is written, rather, from the traditional Christian belief (held by the authors) that such relationships fall short of God's purpose in Creation, and the conviction that, given the predominance of this view for most of Western history, and the support for it in the Judaeo-Christian Scriptures, it will continue to be held by a significant number of people even as many in society, for the time being, move away from it.

The question we seek to address is what forms of pastoral and counselling support can legitimately be offered, by those who hold traditional ethical views, to those who share them and who struggle personally with *unwanted* same-sex attraction.

Neither of us has been involved in formal counselling or 'therapy' with people struggling with same-sex attraction. However, writing as a professor of psychiatry and a lecturer in Christian ethics, and grateful for the input of a number of Christian leaders who share our concerns, we are seeking to respond to two major challenges. First, many who hold to a traditional sexual ethic are increasingly reticent about articulating and commending that ethic, even if they are leaders in churches which officially uphold and teach it. This is, in part, because of the hostility shown by some who oppose them but it is also because they are unsure about how to put their beliefs into practice pastorally.

Secondly, many who reject the traditional ethic are also increasingly vocal and vehement in their opposition to all forms of pastoral and counselling support that are based on it. Careful attention therefore needs to be given to their critique and to developing and defending a robust Christian apologetic in this area.

Introduction

The central claim being advanced here is that there are scientifically defensible and ethically responsible ways of providing support from an orthodox Christian perspective. Such support should, of course, never be imposed on anyone. It should however be available to those wishing to be encouraged in their quest for a chaste life or seeking a change in the strength or direction of their sexual interests.

To deny orthodox Christians and others the freedom to develop and offer such support is to deny those with unwanted same-sex attraction the right to help in living their own lives in accordance with their beliefs. It is also to restrict choices in response to same-sex attraction in a manner which disregards or distorts the evidence about the complex phenomenon of human sexuality.

The paper opens with a brief overview of our context and the variety of pastoral responses, from an orthodox biblical perspective, to unwanted same-sex attraction. It then explores the evidence on the patterning of human sexual desire before proposing a framework for Christian ministry. After completing the paper it was suggested that we summarise its main points and principles for those perhaps less interested in the technical details and we have summed these up in the twelve key points and brief elaborations on them which follow.

Our hope is that this paper will encourage and empower Christians, particularly those in church leadership, who wish to live and minister within the framework of orthodox Christian sexual ethics. We hope, too, that it will also persuade those who do not share those beliefs to recognise the importance, in a liberal society, of allowing others the freedom to hold them and act upon them.

KEY POINTS

1. **Created in God's image, all human beings, regardless of their sexual interests or attractions, are embraced in the inclusive call of the Christian gospel.** All are invited to respond by trusting and following Jesus Christ and so enjoying transformative fellowship with Him and His other followers.

2. **Christians must recognise and repent of making it difficult for those who experience same-sex attraction (SSA), or any other variations of human sexual interests, to hear the good news and to be open about their experience.** Actions which demean, marginalise or bully people, whatever their sexual experience or background, are to be rejected as a violation of the gospel and the way of Jesus Christ.

3. **Those who embrace Christian faith receive the privileges and accept the responsibilities of Christian discipleship.** These responsibilities are rooted in Scripture and in the church's traditional teaching. In relation to sexual issues, God calls us to chastity by abstaining from sexual intimacy in our friendships and remaining faithful to a spouse of the opposite sex in the covenant of marriage. This is the pattern of sexual conduct called for by the gospel and is good news for human flourishing, relational stability, and family and social life.

4. **Those committed to the Christian vision of human flourishing must be prepared to be counter-cultural.** As in other times and places, Christians today need to beware of conforming to their culture where they should be confidently offering it creative alternatives.

5. **For Christians the teachings of our faith rather than secular constructs such as 'gay', 'lesbian', 'fluid' and 'bisexual' provide the organising principles for the integration of mental life and sexual behaviour.** Christians who follow biblical teaching in matters of sexual ethics define their identity in terms of Christ and their faith in him, rather than by the nature of their sexual attractions.

key points

6. **People with unwanted SSA who seek to live in conformity with their beliefs should be free to receive appropriate and responsible practical care and counsel.** Most may choose counselling and pastoral support to maintain, within a Christian ethical framework, the disciplines of chastity. Others may wish to explore the possibility of achieving some degree of change in the strength or direction of unwanted sexual interests.

7. **Experience of change in the strength or direction of one's sexual interests is sometimes possible.** Although the extent of such change will differ between individuals, what is commonly referred to as sexual 'orientation' is not invariably a fixed and enduring characteristic of the human condition, rooted in biological difference and experienced from birth. Whilst some people experience same-sex attraction from their earliest memories of sexual interest, for others sexual desire can be relatively fluid. There are personal narratives of change of sexual 'orientation' reported in both the secular and religious media. When assessing counselling efforts that seek to promote 'change' in the strength, direction, or expression of same-sex desire, the entire range of human sexual experience must therefore be addressed rather than assuming all sexual attraction is always fixed.

8. **No high quality scientifically controlled trials have been carried out on efforts to promote change in sexual 'orientation' and claims for or against the effectiveness of specific approaches must therefore be treated with caution.** 'Sexual Orientation Change Efforts' have provoked passionate opinions on all sides. Various mental health bodies and professional associations have made negative declarations about their desirability and effectiveness. It has been asserted that there is 'no evidence' that efforts to promote change in sexual 'orientation' are effective. Such statements, if allowed to stand unqualified, are potentially misleading. Because no randomised controlled trials have been carried out in this area, it is not possible to assert conclusively whether efforts to promote 'change' are effective or whether they are

not effective. There is no 'cast iron' evidence either way. A balanced and objective assessment would note there are personal reports of change in sexual orientation from within both secular and religious cultures, but that there remains uncertainty about the effectiveness of any particular psychological or counselling approach designed to promote such change. The same is true of 'gay affirmative' therapies that encourage the acceptance and integration of same-sex attraction, although these counselling approaches are readily available and remain unchallenged in secular culture. Uncertainty as to the effectiveness and harm of such 'gay affirmative' therapies is even greater where they are offered to those who, for reasons of religious belief, view acting on such attractions as wrong.

9. **Health and counselling professionals must practise ethically by respecting the religious beliefs and convictions of their clients and exercising due care in distinguishing between fact and personal opinion.** Professional bodies have rightly recognised and repudiated the prejudice and stigma they have shown toward people with SSA in the past. It is crucial that they now avoid replacing that set of prejudices with similar biases against those who hold orthodox religious views about sexual behaviours.

10. **Given the absence of conclusive, high quality, scientifically controlled trials, those offering formal counselling to people with unwanted SSA must exercise considerable caution.** They must follow conventional ethical guidelines in terms of informed consent and show respect for client autonomy and self-determination. When counselling clients with unwanted SSA, harm could result from raising unrealistic expectations or claims that go beyond the available evidence.

11. **People seeking such support must be given the facts as objectively as possible about the various approaches to managing unwanted same-sex desire and then be free to choose for themselves.** Some may seek the freely available 'gay affirmative' counselling modelled

on prevailing secular, rather than Christian, ethical values. This approach gives priority to what has been termed 'organismic' congruence, centred upon a full integration of same-sex interests into an individual's sense of identity. Others will choose to embrace orthodox Christian teaching as the integrating framework for their identity and seek counselling or pastoral support that is correspondingly modelled on its ethical teachings. This approach, the pursuit of 'telic' congruence, gives priority to enabling people to live holistically with their values and goals, including their religious beliefs and perspectives. Their choice, too, should be respected.

12. **Those with unwanted SSA who seek to live within the orthodox boundaries of Christian faith and ethical practitioners who support them deserve our honour, support and respect.** Both groups should be free to act in accordance with their conscientious beliefs without harassment, misrepresentation or discrimination.

1. The context and the challenge

1.1 The development of a Christian understanding and response to the experience of same-sex attraction is a critical challenge facing the church today. It is particularly pressing for Christians who seek to hold the view that God's call for us all is to live chaste lives by abstaining from sexual intimacy in our friendships and being faithful to a spouse of the opposite sex if we are called to marriage. The challenge here comes in three main forms.

1.2 First, such a view can perpetuate a context in which those who experience same-sex attraction (SSA) are unable to be honest about their experience. They can fear rejection, ridicule, discrimination and prejudice. Such a culture is antithetical to the gospel of truth, freedom and grace. It is therefore vital that we repent of our part in creating it and work to remove it from both church and society.

1.3 Second, as part of its wider rejection of the Christian vision for human flourishing, our society increasingly encourages those who experience same-sex attraction (SSA) to:

- accept such desires
- identify as 'gay', 'lesbian' or 'bisexual' (or 'questioning') and
- explore their sexuality through sexual relationships.

Orthodox Christians wish to offer an alternative path consistent with the traditional teaching of the Christian faith. This understands such desires as falling short of God's purpose in creation. It therefore rejects affirmation of same-sex sexual relationships. The articulation of such an alternative vision is often now viewed as inherently oppressive and denying basic human rights. The only acceptable counselling is held to be 'gay affirmative'. This is counselling in which lesbian, gay and bisexual lifestyles are regarded positively, and the acknowledgment and expression of same-sex desire in the process of identity development is given priority.[1,2] Christians (and those of other faiths) need, however, to be free to teach and model a counter-cultural vision for human relationships rooted in the will and purpose of God.

1.4 Third, there are particular issues raised in relation to Christian discipleship, pastoral care and counselling for those, whether married or single, who experience same-sex attraction (SSA) and seek to live chaste lives. People must be able to find wise Christian counsel and support.[3] The church as a whole needs to be free and equipped to support and guide them and to offer viable alternatives to 'gay affirmative' counselling.

The variety of alternatives to 'gay affirmative' counselling

1.5 Alternatives to affirmation of same-sex sexual relationships take a variety of forms. It is important to recognise this diversity and the differences of approach among those who support Christians seeking to order their lives in accordance with traditional Christian teaching.

1.6 There is a diversity of *people* offering counsel and support. These include:

- those who, as Christian leaders and fellow disciples in the context of a church fellowship, pray and walk with people out of pastoral concern [4]

- those who, through organisations and networks, offer structured support groups for Christians struggling with unwanted same-sex attraction [5]

- those who, as Christian counsellors and psychotherapists, offer more professional interventions aiming to assist processes of change in the strength or direction of sexual attractions. This is what the American Psychological Association has called Sexual

Orientation Change Efforts (SOCE), a phrase adopted below despite legitimate questions about the terminology of 'sexual orientation'[6,7]

1.7 There is a spectrum of *outcomes* sought or offered which broadly ranges between these two poles:

- forms of behavioural control over unwanted feelings of same-sex attraction in order to strengthen chaste behaviour corresponding with a person's religious convictions (for example, ceasing use of pornography or ending promiscuous patterns of sexual behaviour)

- change in the pattern of sexual feelings by seeking a diminishing of same-sex attraction or an increase in opposite sex attraction

Broadly speaking, all pastors would want to find ways of supporting the former whereas the latter is more likely to require trained counsellors.

1.8 There is a variety of *foundations* for providing support. The two most common bases would be:

- a theological belief about God's intention for sexual relationships

- more theory-driven conceptualisations of sexual development and the origins of same-sex attraction and how to change such attraction

1.9 In articulating principles of good practice across this range of responses, it is important to stress that the experience of SSA *per se* is not something for which individuals are personally blameworthy. Seeking and offering assistance to help alter the strength or direction of such attraction is fully compatible with the traditional Christian sexual ethic but it is not the only form of pastoral care and support the church should offer. It is therefore wrong to insist that all Christians who experience SSA must follow a path focused on changing unwanted same-sex attractions as opposed to a more limited goal focused on maintaining chaste behaviour. *It is, however, equally wrong that those people who wish to explore the possibility of achieving change in the strength or direction of unwanted SSA are denied the freedom to explore that path.*

1.10 What is needed, therefore, is:

- an understanding of the current evidence on the nature and patterning of human sexual desire (section 2)

- a framework for Christian ministry (section 3). This needs to:

    - recognise the potential benefits, limits, and risks involved in seeking to help people who seek to change their experience of, and response to, SSA and

    - provide a number of principles to guide those offering to help in this way

2. Summary of evidence on the patterning of human sexual desires

2.1 Issues of SSA need to be set in the context of the wider reality that human sexual interests vary along a number of different dimensions. These include a range of preferences for different kinds of sexual activity and differences in the types of people to whom we are sexually attracted.[8, 9] *Variation of sexual interest in terms of the sex/gender of the people one is attracted to is only one part of this more complex phenomenon.*

2.2 All variations in the patterning of human sexual desire are likely to result from a developmental interaction between biological (including genetic) factors, environmental factors and the influence of personal human agency. This includes whether one is attracted to those of the same sex, opposite sex, or both sexes.[10] As with most complex human behaviours, our understanding of the relative contributions of these different factors is poor. Furthermore, their respective contributions will vary between individuals. We still have a great deal to learn about how sexual behaviours vary across cultures, how they fluctuate through childhood and adolescence and the influences of cultural and social factors on early sexual development. Attempts to understand these variations are currently hampered by the poor quality of much research and the methodological problems of collecting information from large and representative samples using valid measures.[11]

2.3 Caution is therefore needed about drawing conclusions from available data concerning the causes of different patterns of sexual desire. In particular this means that:

- simplistic explanatory paradigms that try to reduce differences of sexual interest to 'choice' or 'biology' should be avoided

- there are dangers in insisting any single model is adequate to explain all experience of same-sex attraction and thus able to help every individual wishing to change such attraction

2. Summary of evidence on the patterning of human sexual desires

- the old binary divisions of 'heterosexual' and 'homosexual' need to be challenged.[12, 13] While people may choose, for a variety of reasons, to identify themselves in terms of such categories ('gay' or 'straight'), they do not correspond with any clear-cut biological differences. Furthermore, there is no reliable scientific evidence that, in all individuals, such variations are necessarily 'fixed' biologically at birth

2.4 Sexual attractions are better understood as lying on a spectrum rather than in terms of a simple dichotomous binary categorisation. Survey data suggest that mixed patterns of sexual desire, including attraction to both sexes at the same time, appear to be more common than exclusive SSA, especially among women.[14, 15] This is particularly so once variation in sexual attraction over time is considered. The best evidence[16, 17, 18] suggests that only a very small percentage of men (1-2%) and women (0.5-1.5%) experience *exclusive* same-sex attraction throughout their life course. It appears that more men and women experience *mixed* patterns of sexual interest. This includes shifts of interest from one sex to another at various points in their lives or attractions to both sexes at the same time.[19]

2.5 Debates about the ethical and moral implications of sexuality and discussions about the possibility of change of 'sexual orientation' have regrettably focused on the small minority of those with exclusive and enduring same-sex attraction. This is not to underestimate their importance. Nevertheless, any consideration of the morality of same-sex behaviour in relation to the ethical requirements of Christian belief, or the possibility of 'change' of sexual interest, must also address the much larger group for whom sexual desire is experienced as more 'plastic' and flexible.

2.6 In addition to survey evidence, there are now numerous convincing personal narratives of change in patterns of sexual interest from within both secular and religious communities.[20] Although various explanations for such change have been offered, our understandings about the causes and mechanisms are limited.[21] It is particularly difficult to identify factors that might promote or deter changing sexual interests in any one individual. Anecdotal evidence suggests that, for some, change may be experienced as occurring spontaneously; for others, a change in philosophical perspective, or personal religious conviction, appears to play a cardinal role.[22]

3. A framework for Christian ministry among people with unwanted same-sex attraction

3.1 The Christian faith contains (as do many other faiths) a great deal of teaching about the moral ordering of sexual behaviours.[23] Orthodox Christians believe the moral framework set out in the Christian scriptures and the traditional teaching of the Church is God's will for the well-being of all people and that as believers they are called to order their own sexual behaviour within this framework. This is their calling regardless of the precise nature or causes of different human sexual interests and regardless of the degree to which these may be experienced as 'fixed' or as relatively flexible.

3.2 Christians recognise that all people have a responsibility to choose how they respond to this traditional teaching. Some will choose to reject it and instead pursue patterns of life that correspond with their prevailing sexual interests. Others, however, will choose their Christian belief as the organising principle for the governance of their sexual behaviour. It is the support and affirmation of this second group that concerns us here.

3.3 As noted earlier, there are many forms of Christian ministry to those with same-sex attraction who wish to live in accordance with traditional Christian teaching. It is indisputable that more specific therapy-based efforts (Sexual Orientation Change Efforts (SOCE)) have provoked controversy in recent years. Professional organisations in the field of counselling, psychology and psychiatry have expressed concern about their desirability and effectiveness.[24,25]

3.4 Efforts by these professional organisations to evaluate the benefits and potential harms of all therapeutic approaches offered within their speciality areas and to ensure that their members conform to the highest standards of professional behaviour must be supported and affirmed. Christians offering ministries or counselling, especially in the form of seeking to change patterns of sexual interest, must also demonstrate a concern for truthful evaluation of the evidence and for preventing harm in their ministries.

3. A framework for Christian ministry among people with unwanted same-sex attraction

3.5 Similarly, efforts by professional organisations to acknowledge their own histories of prejudice and discrimination against people with SSA deserve support and affirmation from everyone. It is critically important however that these organisations should now be vigilant to new forms of prejudice and discrimination within their ranks. These can develop against people of Christian faith, and those of other faiths, who hold traditional moral values in relation to the governance of sexual desire.

3.6 Another development to be welcomed is the growing recognition among secular counsellors that they must be sensitive to, and respect, their clients' faith and beliefs and must not seek to impose their own beliefs in the therapeutic process. In the field of medicine, for example, the UK General Medical Council has issued guidance that states that doctors must *'respect patients' right to hold religious or other beliefs and should take those beliefs into account where they may be relevant to treatment'*.[26] It is important that this includes their clients' convictions regarding the moral ordering of sexual interests. Here, too, all counsellors and therapists must respect the autonomy and convictions of their clients.[27]

3.7 In a recent report[28] addressing this matter of SOCE, the American Psychological Association (APA) developed an important distinction. They contrasted two basic philosophical approaches that clients may adopt in response to their experience of SSA, depending upon their personal moral convictions. The first is affirmative of SSA. It gives priority to what has been termed *'organismic'* congruence – seeking a sense of wholeness in one's experiential self. This approach pursues the full integration of same-sex interests into an individual's sense of identity and lifestyle. The APA recognises, however, an alternative approach which they label as the pursuit of *'telic'* congruence. This too offers an approach that seeks to be holistic and enable the flourishing of individuals. It does so by giving priority to enabling people to live consistently with their own goals, including their religious perspectives

3. A framework for Christian ministry among people with unwanted same-sex attraction

and values. This approach, when faced with individuals whose religious beliefs lead to tensions with their sexual attractions, will respect those clients who choose to give priority to their beliefs and values as the organising principle for their sense of identity and management of their behaviour.

3.8 Pursuing this distinction further, clients seeking 'organismic' congruence may choose to pursue 'gay affirmative' counselling approaches. These counselling approaches attempt to support identity development and integration by giving precedence to the acknowledgement and expression of the client's prevailing sexual interests and desires. Their right to do this must be respected. However, it must be noted that outcomes associated with these affirmative counselling approaches have not been reliably researched and there is little robust evidence for their effectiveness, [29] especially in relation to outcomes among those with unwanted same-sex attractions and conflicting religious beliefs.

3.9 Clients seeking 'telic' congruence may alternatively wish to explore 'faith-affirmative' counselling approaches. These approaches attempt to support identity development and integration that gives precedence to the client's religious beliefs and convictions regarding the ordering of their sexual interests and behaviours. Orthodox Christians, as a result of their faith commitments, will choose to reject behavioural expression of same-sex sexual desire in favour of obedience to precepts of their faith. A commitment to uphold the right of freedom of religion entails that they have a basic right to make such choices and to be supported in them.

3.10 As noted above (1.5-1.8), a diversity of approaches seek to support those wishing to live consistently within the traditional Christian moral framework for human flourishing. All of these approaches, ranging from simple prayer and friendship, through to more specific therapy-based interventions, are offered to those seeking telic congruence. However, as noted above (3.3), more specific therapy-based interventions (SOCE) that attempt to change patterns of orientation have attracted controversy.

3. A framework for Christian ministry among people with unwanted same-sex attraction

This controversy revolves around three areas of SOCE that are often confused: their desirability (3.11), effectiveness (3.12-16) and potential for harm (3.17). *These three issues should be addressed separately.*

3.11 First, it is frequently argued that such efforts are undesirable in principle because they perpetuate the 'pathologisation' of SSA.[30] We acknowledge that same-sex behaviour is no longer regarded as a disease or disorder. It must be recognised, however, that there is a fundamental difference of view about the *moral* status of same-sex behaviours and therefore the desirability of seeking change. All Christians are called to a personal journey of transformation and the resources of the biological and behavioural sciences are among God's gifts for the pursuit of human flourishing. It is quite possible to harness these resources, alongside the spiritual resources of the Christian faith, in pursuit of growth and change without resorting to concepts of sickness. Questions about the pathological status of same-sex behaviours must not however be conflated with questions about whether efforts to change actually 'work'.

3.12 Second, when considering the relative effectiveness of SOCE it is important to note that professional counselling, psychology and psychiatry organisations are ethically obligated to review scientific evidence dispassionately and to present their findings fairly and objectively. Where there is insufficient high quality evidence their advice to their members, and to the general public, must reflect a fair and dispassionate appraisal of what evidence is available. In particular they must distinguish between a fair evaluation of the available scientific data and the promotion of their own religious or philosophical beliefs under the guise of their professional status.

3.13 The strongest evidence for the effectiveness of a particular counselling or therapy approach is provided from randomised, controlled trials (RCT's). However, for many commonly available counselling approaches, including both 'gay affirmative' (or organismic) and 'faith affirmative' (or telic congruence) counselling approaches noted above, evidence of this quality is not available.[32] This is because of logistical hurdles, resource constraints, or difficulties in maintaining placebo-controlled conditions. In such circumstances individual practitioners usually evaluate the evidence available from less rigorous sources such as anecdotal case reports, outcomes measured in case-series and data from non-randomised trials. They then attempt to balance the potential benefits against potential risks.[33, 34]

3.14 The generally accepted convention in evaluating under-researched and unproven counselling and psychotherapy approaches is that 'absence of evidence is not evidence of absence'.[35] In other words, the fact that there is no evidence of an effect is not evidence of no effect. It is often asserted that 'there is no evidence that SOCE work'. This is true, in the sense that no RCT's have been conducted in this area. *But this does not mean that we have evidence that SOCE do not work.* We simply do not know whether they work or whether they do not work.[36]

3.15 In the case of SOCE, because of the absence of high quality evidence we are required to make a judgment based upon lower quality evidence such as data from individual case studies (or outcomes in case series). We must then balance the potential benefits against potential harm. As we have noted, this is the case for some other counselling approaches, including 'gay affirmative' therapy offered to those who hold orthodox faith convictions.

3.16 The available data suggest that some individuals report benefit in the form of increased heterosexual interest and/or marked reduction in same-sex interest after participating in one of these approaches.[37, 38] Because of the absence of controlled experiments we do not know whether, regardless of a particular therapy approach, these changes would have happened anyway. Nor do we know whether it is the particular approach, as opposed to a general placebo effect, that has been effective. Nevertheless, despite our lack of knowledge about the

3. A framework for Christian ministry among people with unwanted same-sex attraction

mechanisms of change, there are undoubtedly individuals who have reported significant changes in the strength or direction of their sexual attraction either spontaneously or as a result of participating in some form of SOCE.

3.17 Third, it has been claimed that SOCE cause harm. As with all counselling or therapeutic interventions, SOCE have the potential to cause harm. This is especially so where expectations are not managed or are unrealistic and where there is poor training and supervision. The current evidence about harm is mixed: some surveys [39] report significant numbers whereas in others the prevalence of harm is absent or negligible. [40] These differences are likely to reflect biases in the methodology. As we have noted, no high quality RCT's have been carried out in this area. Thus, assertions that SOCE cause harm rely upon anecdotal data, small case series and potentially biased surveys. In the absence of controlled experiments, we do not know whether, regardless of a particular therapy approach, these 'harmful' experiences would have occurred anyway. More research is needed into the possible harmful side effects of different approaches. Meanwhile, where individuals wish to explore the possibility of change through some form of SOCE, the *potential* for harm can be minimised by:

- careful attention to the management of expectations

- the provision of accurate information and

- careful adherence to other safeguards outlined below

3.18 Considering the three issues of desirability, effectiveness and potential harm separately, if orthodox Christians believe that it is desirable to explore the possibility of change, then it is reasonable to support their right and ability to make that choice. Given the evidence summarised above that SOCE can sometimes be effective and do not necessarily harm, there are no compelling reasons, subject to safeguards, why those who desire to do so should be prevented or deterred from cautiously exploring the possibility of change through participation in one or other form of SOCE.

A way forward

3.19 It is important to defend the right of Christian believers, and those from other faith traditions, to seek prayer ministry or pastoral and counselling support to control unwanted sexual behaviours, within the moral framework of their religious convictions. For many people with longer term patterns of SSA the goal of such support may be the nurture of the disciplines of celibacy.

3.20 In offering such support, ministers must follow conventional guidelines for all such pastoral ministry. [41] In particular, they must:

- avoid raising unrealistic expectations

- respect the autonomy and conscientious judgments of those to whom they minister

- seek appropriate supervision for their own practice and professional behaviour.

3.21 Those offering more explicit SOCE face further particular ethical obligations. It is important that therapists follow conventional professional guidelines, especially in terms of respecting client autonomy, the avoidance of prejudice and stigma, and presenting the available evidence fairly and objectively. [42, 43] It must also be recognised that there is insufficient evidence to estimate the strength of any effect associated with a particular therapy base. Given the public interest in these matters, it is additionally important that counsellors and therapists give detailed information about the nature, potential harm and the proposed benefits of counselling approaches. Finally, it is crucial that prospective clients are able to give fully informed consent, that their consent is recorded, and that professionals follow usual professional standards of conduct in terms of training requirements, supervision of their work, and a commitment to further evaluation and research.

4. Conclusion

4.1 In the words of the important St Andrew's Day Statement of 1995, 'The interpretation of homosexual emotion and behaviour is a Christian "task", still inadequately addressed. "Guided by God's Spirit", the church must be open to empirical observation and governed by the authority of the apostolic testimony... Many competing interpretations of the phenomena can be found in contemporary discussion, none of them with an unchallengeable basis in scientific data. The church has no need to espouse any one theory, but may learn from many'. [44] As the Church undertakes this interpretive task and learns from competing interpretations, it is important for the sake of its pastoral care and its mission that it does so with intellectual integrity and in a manner that respects the image of God in all people and reflects the character of Christ.

4.2 Our society is increasingly unconvinced by traditional Christian teaching and can be hostile to those who express and act on such beliefs. In such a context it is important that Christians do not lose their confidence to minister in accordance with biblical teaching. Nor should they become so defensive that they cease to be self-critical and fail to protect themselves against misguided and potentially harmful approaches.

4.3 This booklet has, in response to these challenges, outlined the range of approaches the Church can offer to those seeking to live according to orthodox Christian teaching. It has also demonstrated that these, including forms of SOCE, are fully consistent with the current evidence about the patterning of human sexual desires. Finally, it has set out the integrity of a position which, with various important safeguards, enables people to live and to flourish according to their Christian beliefs and convictions.

REFERENCES

1. There is no clear definition of 'gay affirmative therapy'. Some authors simply use the term to mean that a therapist views LGBT identity and sexual relationships positively and would not attempt to diminish experience of SSA; for others it describes a more theory-driven integration into identity of felt sexual preferences.
2. Ritter K, Terndrup AI. *Handbook of Affirmative Psychotherapy with Lesbians and Gay Men.* New York: Guilford Press, 2002
3. Haldeman DC. When Sexual and Religious Orientation Collide: Considerations in Working with Conflicted Same-Sex Attracted Male Clients. *The Counseling Psychologist* 2004; 32 (5): 691-715
4. Helpful resources here include Tylee A. *Walking with Gay Friends: A Journey of Informed Compassion.* IVP, 2007 and Yarhouse MA. *Homosexuality and the Christian: A Guide for Parents, Pastors, and Friends.* Baker, 2010
5. True Freedom Trust is one of several such organisation in the United Kingdom. www.truefreedomtrust.co.uk
6. See 2009 Report of the APA Task Force on Appropriate Therapeutic Responses to Sexual Orientation. Available online at www.apa.org/pi/lgbt/resources/sexual-orientation.aspx
7. Goddard A, Harrison G. Changing Sexual Orientation and Identity? A Critique of the APA Report. 2009. Available online at www.fulcrum-anglican.org.uk/page.cfm?ID=475
8. Stein E. *The Mismeasure of Desire: The Science, Theory, and Ethics of Sexual Orientation.* Oxford: Oxford University Press, 1999: 61-70
9. Moser C, Kleinplatz PJ. Dsm-Iv-Tr and the Paraphilias: An Argument for Removal. *J Psychol Hum Sex* 2005; 17 (3/4): 91-109. Available online at bit.ly/pC64qa
10. De Pomerai D. Biological Mechanisms in Homosexuality: A Critical Review. In ed Groves P. *The Anglican Communion and Homosexuality: A Resource to Enable Listening and Dialogue.* London: SPCK, 2008: 268-92
11. The literature is reviewed comprehensively in Harrison G. 'Unwanted Same-sex Attractions: Can Pastoral and Counselling Interventions Help People to Change?' In ed Groves P. *The Anglican Communion and Homosexuality: A Resource to Enable Listening and Dialogue.* London: SPCK, 2008: 293-332
12. The American Psychological Association's Guidelines for Psychotherapy with Lesbian, Gay and Bisexual Clients encourage psychologists to adopt a more complex understanding of sexual orientation rather than a 'dichotomous model' in their approach to treatment. Available online at bit.ly/qjJcYp
13. Matteson D. Counseling and Psychotherapy with Bisexual and Exploring Clients. In ed Firestein B. *Bisexuality: The Psychology and Politics of an Invisible Minority.* Newbury Park, CA: Sage Publications, 1996: 185-213
14. Bailey J, Dunne MP, Martin N. Genetic and Environmental Influences on Sexual Orientation and Its Correlates in an Australian Twin Sample. *J Pers Soc Psychol* 2000; 78: 524-36
15. Santtila P et al. Potential for Homosexual Response Is Prevalent and Genetic. *Biol Psychol* 2008; 77 (1): 102-5
16. Dickson N, Paul C, Herbison P. Same-Sex Attraction in a Birth Cohort: Prevalence and Persistence in Early Adulthood. *Soc Sci Med* 2003; 56 (8): 1607-15
17. Laumann EO, Gagnon JH, Michael RT, Michaels S. *The Social Organization of Sexuality: Sexual Practices in the United States.* Chicago: University of Chicago Press, 1994
18. Savin-Williams RC, Ream GL. Prevalence and Stability of Sexual Orientation Components During Adolescence and Young Adulthood. *Arch Sex Behav* 2007; 36: 385-94
19. Kinnish KK, Strassberg DS, Turner CW. Sex Differences in the Flexibility of Sexual Orientation: A Multidimensional Retrospective Assessment. *Arch Sex Behav* 2005; 34 (2): 173-83
20. For example, the human rights campaigner Peter Tatchell has said: 'If we are all born either gay or straight, how do they explain people who switch in mid-life from fulfilled heterosexuality to fulfilled homosexuality (and vice versa) ...In an enlightened, gay-affirming society, more people might be inclined to explore same-sex desire'. Available online at www.guardian.co.uk/commentisfree/2006/jun/28/borngayormadegay (accessed September 2011)

    The journalist Matthew Parris has written 'I think sexuality is a supple as well as subtle thing, and can sometimes be influenced, even promoted; I think that in some people some drives can be discouraged and others encouraged; I think some people can choose. I wish I were conscious of being able to. I would choose to be gay' Available online at thetim.es/lQlbFi (accessed September 2011)
21. Harrison G. Unwanted Same-sex Attractions: Can Pastoral and Counselling Interventions Help People to Change? In ed Groves P. *The Anglican Communion and Homosexuality: A Resource to Enable Listening and Dialogue.* London: SPCK, 2008: 293-332

22. For example, Sue Wilkinson, Professor of Feminist and Health Studies at Loughborough University, UK, reportedly said: 'I was never unsure about my sexuality throughout my teens or 20s. I was a happy heterosexual and had no doubts. Then I changed, through political activity and feminism, spending time with women's organisations. It opened my mind to the possibility of a lesbian identity.' (bit.ly/pyHtzj) Similarly, Jacky Clune documented her experience in an article in the Daily Mail 26 June 2010 'How I went from committed lesbian to a happily married mother of four' (bit.ly/duUvK8). There are also numerous anecdotes of change in the context of orthodox religious faith and conviction eg bit.ly/c53RYi
23. Official Roman Catholic Teaching is found in the Catechism of the Catholic Church, for example, Part 3, Section 2, Chapter 2, Article 6 on the commandment against adultery. The Anglican Communion's teaching is summarised in Resolution I.10 of the 1998 Lambeth Conference
24. bit.ly/n8izgo
25. bit.ly/dvC2c
26. bit.ly/9FmQ1Y
27. Haldeman DC. When Sexual and Religious Orientation Collide: Considerations in Working with Conflicted Same-Sex Attracted Male Clients. *The Counseling Psychologist* 2004; 32 (5): 691-715
28. See 2009 Report of the APA Task Force on Appropriate Therapeutic Responses to Sexual Orientation. Available online at www.apa.org/pi/lgbt/resources/sexual-orientation.aspx
29. King M et al. *A Systematic Review of Research on Counselling and Psychotherapy for Lesbian, Gay, Bisexual and Transgender People*. British Association for Counselling and Psychotherapy, 2007. Available online at www.bacp.co.uk/research/LGBT_web.pdf
30. bit.ly/putohO
31. See, for example, the guidance from the UK General Medical Council. Available online at bit.ly/9FmQ1Y
32. King M et al. *A Systematic Review of Research on Counselling and Psychotherapy for Lesbian, Gay, Bisexual and Transgender People*. British Association for Counselling and Psychotherapy, 2007. Available online at www.bacp.co.uk/research/LGBT_web.pdf
33. See 2009 Report of the APA Task Force on Appropriate Therapeutic Responses to Sexual Orientation. Available online at www.apa.org/pi/lgbt/resources/sexual-orientation.aspx
34. Centre for Reviews and Dissemination. *Undertaking Systematic Reviews of Research on Effectiveness: CRD's Guidance for Carrying out or Commissioning Reviews*, Centre for Reviews and Dissemination Report 4. University of York, 2001. Current edition available online at www.york.ac.uk/inst/crd/index_guidance.htm
35. Altman DG, Bland JM. Statistics Notes: Absence of Evidence Is Not Evidence of Absence. *BMJ* 1995; 311: 485. Available online at www.bmj.com/content/311/7003/485.full
36. In philosophical logic, this is also known as argumentum ad ignorantiam, or appeal to ignorance. It is considered an informal logical fallacy because it asserts that a proposition is necessarily true because it has not been proved false (or vice versa). See, for example, Madsen P. *How to Win Every Argument: The Use and Abuse of Logic*. London: Continuum, 2006
37. Spitzer R. Can Some Gay Men and Lesbians Change Their Sexual Orientation? 200 Participants Reporting a Change from Homosexual to Heterosexual Orientation. *Arch Sex Behav* 2003; 32 (5): 403-17
38. Jones SL, Yarhouse MA. *Ex-Gays?: A Longitudinal Study of Religiously Mediated Change in Sexual Orientation*. Downers Grove, Ill.: IVP Academic, 2007
39. Shidlo A, Schroeder M. Changing Sexual Orientation: A Consumers' Report. *Prof Psychol-Res Pr* 2002; 33: 249-59
40. Jones SL, Yarhouse MA. *Ex-Gays?: A Longitudinal Study of Religiously Mediated Change in Sexual Orientation*. Downers Grove, Ill.: IVP Academic, 2007
41. For example Church of England General Synod. *Guidelines for the Professional Conduct of the Clergy*. London: Church House Publishing, 2003. Available online at bit.ly/paeAJW
42. The recent review (2009) of SOCE by the American Psychological Association cited favourably the Sexual Identity Therapy Framework (2006) of Throckmorton W and Yarhouse M as a means of clients addressing conflicting religious and sexual issues within a therapeutic framework. For information on their framework. Available online at bit.ly/oGLz5n
43. Professional conduct guidelines vary according to professional group but those for doctors are available at bit.ly/njae6a and for counsellors the BACP offers guidance. Available online at www.bacp.co.uk/prof_conduct
44. bit.ly/qYJXJi